PLANETS

VENUS

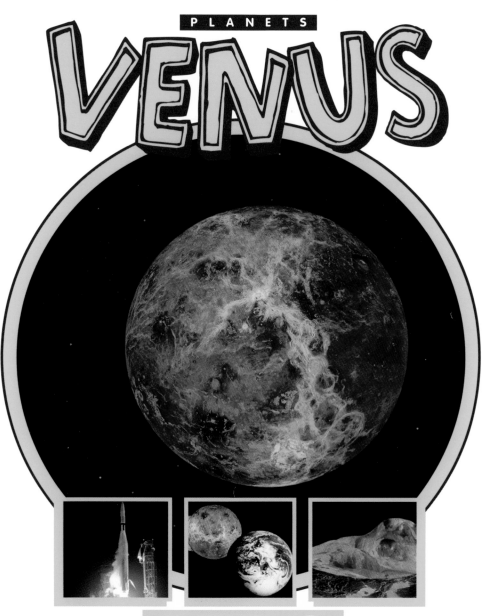

ABDO
Publishing Company

A Buddy Book by Fran Howard

VISIT US AT

www.abdopublishing.com

Published by ABDO Publishing Company, 8000 West 78th Street, Edina, Minnesota 55439.

Printed in the United States.

Editor: Sarah Tieck
Contributing Editor: Michael P. Goecke
Graphic Design: Maria Hosley
Cover Image(s): Lushpix.
Interior Images: Library of Congress (page 23); Lushpix (page 11, 16); NASA: Ames Research Center (page 30), Headquarters—Greatest Images Of NASA (page 25), Jet Propulsion Laboratory (page 6–7, 12, 13, 28, 29), Kennedy Space Center (page 27), Johnson Space Center (page 9, 27); Photodisc (page 5); Photos.com (page 15); SHdigital (page 21).

Library of Congress Cataloging-in-Publication Data

Howard, Fran.
  Venus / Fran Howard.
     p. cm. -- (The planets)
  Includes index.
  ISBN 978-1-59928-824-6
  1. Venus (Planet)--Juvenile literature. I. Title.

  QB621.H69 2008
  523.42--dc22

                                        2007014761

Table Of Contents

The Planet Venus

Venus is a planet. A planet is a large body in space.

Planets travel around stars. The path a planet travels is its orbit. When the planet circles a star, it is orbiting the star.

The sun is a star. Venus orbits the sun. The sun's gravity holds Venus in place as it circles. Venus orbits the sun in about 225 Earth days.

Venus is slightly smaller than Earth.

Our Solar System

OUTER PLANETS

Neptune ————————————

     Uranus ————————

       Saturn ——————

        Jupiter ————

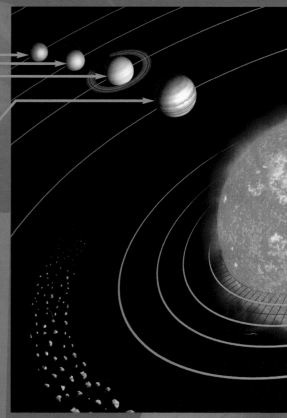

Venus is one of several planets that orbit our sun. The planets orbiting the sun make up our solar system. Our solar system has eight major planets.

The other planets in our solar system are Mercury, Earth, Mars, Jupiter, Saturn, Uranus, and Neptune.

Venus is about 67 million miles (108 million km) from the sun. It is the second-closest planet in our solar system to the sun.

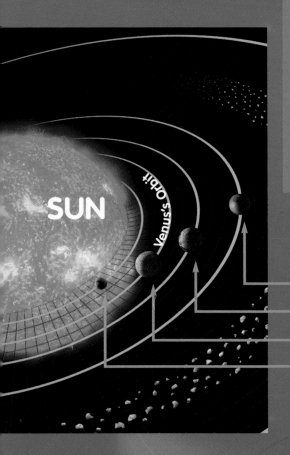

SUN

Venus's Orbit

Mars

Earth

Venus

Mercury

INNER PLANETS

A Bright Planet

Venus is very bright in Earth's sky. In fact, Venus is brighter than the brightest star. Sometimes it can even be seen in the middle of the day!

Sometimes planets such as Venus and Mars *(above)* are so bright that they appear to glow. But unlike stars, planets do not glow. Light from the sun reflects off a planet's surface.

A View Of Venus

Volcanoes cover the surface of Venus. Venus has more volcanoes than Earth!

Venus has 167 giant volcanoes. Each of these is more than 62 miles (100 km) across.

About 1,000 basins cover Venus. These basins are sometimes called craters. They were created when large space objects hit Venus.

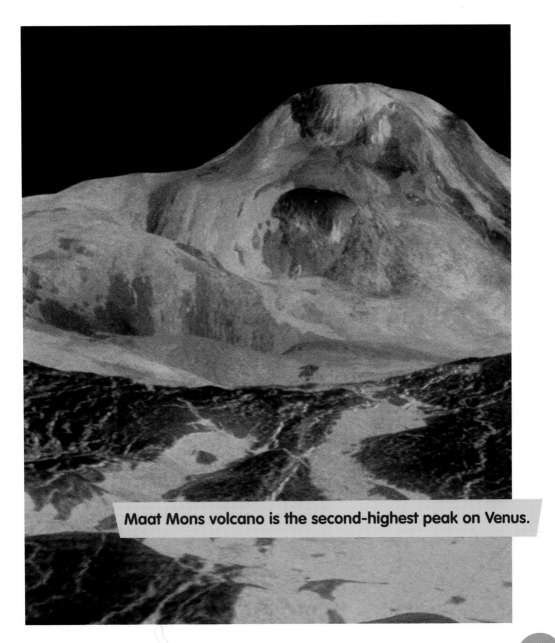

Maat Mons volcano is the second-highest peak on Venus.

It isn't easy to see the surface of Venus. This is because its sky is full of clouds.

Venus is windy, too! There are strong winds at the top of Venus's cloud layer. The winds circle the planet every four to five days.

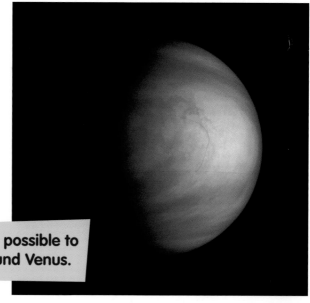

Even from far away, it is possible to see winds swirling around Venus.

Venus has two high land areas called continents. One of the continents is called Ishtar. The other is called Aphrodite Terra. These continents are not surrounded by water.

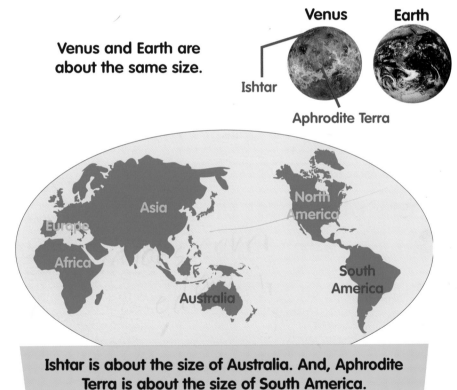

Venus and Earth are about the same size.

Venus   **Earth**

Ishtar

Aphrodite Terra

Ishtar is about the size of Australia. And, Aphrodite Terra is about the size of South America.

What Is It Like There?

Layers of gases surround each planet. These layers are a planet's **atmosphere**.

The atmosphere on Venus is made mostly of **carbon dioxide**. This gas traps heat. So, temperatures on Venus can reach 880 degrees Fahrenheit (470°C)!

Venus is the hottest planet. Humans could not live there. It is too hot. Temperatures on Venus are hot enough to melt lead. And, Venus's temperatures do not change much.

Scientists believe that Venus once had water. This water would have been similar to Earth's oceans. Some scientists think the water disappeared as Venus grew hotter.

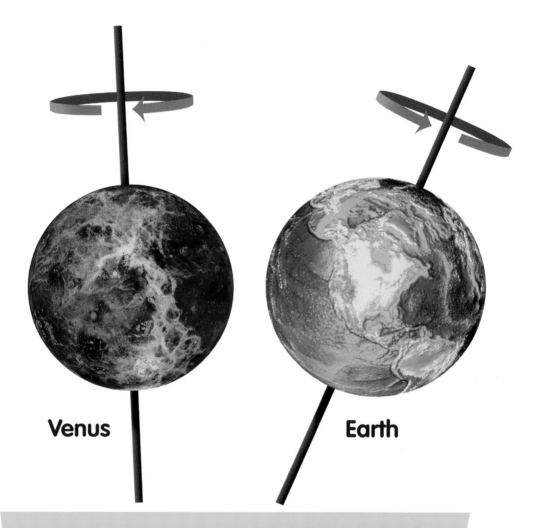

Venus

Earth

Venus spins in the opposite direction of Earth. It is the only
planet to spin in a different direction than its orbit.

Planets spin on an **axis**. This spinning creates night and day. Day occurs on the side of the planet facing the sun. Night occurs on the side facing away from the sun.

Most of the planets in our solar system spin in the same direction as they orbit. However, Venus spins in the opposite direction. It is the only planet to spin this way.

Venus spins very slowly. It takes Venus 243 Earth days to make one complete spin.

Beneath The Surface

The planet Venus has three layers. There is a core, a mantle, and a crust.

The core is the center layer. Venus's core is mostly iron.

The mantle lies between the core and the crust. Venus's mantle is made of hot, melted rock.

The crust is the outer layer. It covers the surface of the planet.

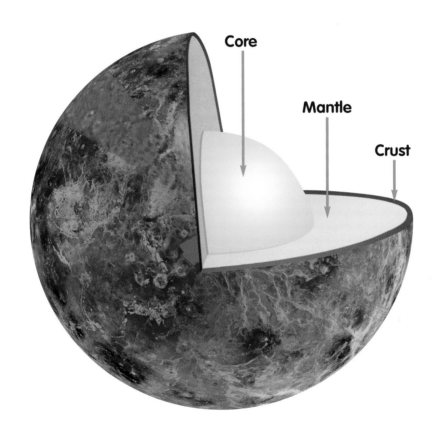

Core

Mantle

Crust

Discovering Venus

Venus is easily seen in Earth's sky. Its clouds reflect almost all of the sun's light back into space. Since Venus is so easy to see, it was known in ancient times.

The Romans named Venus after their goddess of love. It is the only planet named after a goddess. All the other planets are named after gods.

Venus rises and sets with the sun. So, ancient people thought Venus was two different stars. They were called the "Morning Star" and the "Evening Star."

Italian scientist Galileo was the first person to see Venus through a telescope. That was in the early 1600s. In 1790, Johann Schröter discovered Venus's **atmosphere**.

Galileo was a scientist and a philosopher. He made many discoveries that are important to science today.

Missions To Venus

In the 1960s, the United States and the Soviet Union started a race. They wanted to see who could learn the most about Venus first.

From 1961 to 1983, the Soviets sent 16 *Venera* probes to Venus.

The United States sent ten probes to Venus. These were called the *Mariner* spacecraft.

The *Mariner 1* spacecraft lifted off in 1962.

In 1989, the United States launched the *Magellan* **probe**. This probe mapped nearly the entire surface of Venus!

All of these **missions** helped scientists learn more about Venus.

Magellan orbited Venus
to collect information.

The *Magellan* probe launched
inside the orbiter *Atlantis*.

Fact Trek

Because Venus and Earth are close to the same size, they are often called sister planets.

The symbol for Venus is a circle on top of a *t*. This is the same symbol used for the female gender.

The highest mountain on Venus is Maxwell Montes. It is higher than Mount Everest, the tallest mountain on Earth.

Into The Future

People continue to explore space. They want to learn more about Venus.

In November 2005, the European Space Agency launched a space probe to Venus. This probe is called the *Venus Express*. In April 2006, it began orbiting Venus. It gathered information about the planet's atmosphere.

Japan plans to launch a mission to Venus in 2010.

Missions to Venus give scientists more information about the planet.

Important Words

atmosphere the layer of gases that surrounds a planet.

axis an imaginary line through a planet. Planets spin around this line.

carbon dioxide a gas made of carbon and oxygen. People and animals breathe out this gas.

gravity the force that draws things toward a planet and prevents them from floating away. Stars use this force to keep planets in their orbit.

mission the sending of spacecraft to perform specific jobs.

probe a spacecraft that attempts to gather information.

spacecraft a vehicle that travels in space.

volcano a mountain with hot liquid rock at its center.

Web Sites

To learn more about **Venus**, visit ABDO Publishing Company on the World Wide Web. Web sites about **Venus** are featured on our Book Links page. These links are routinely monitored and updated to provide the most current information available.

www.abdopublishing.com

INDEX